A RICH MAN IN POOR CLOTHES

The Story of St. Francis of Assisi Biography Books for Kids 9-12 | Children's Biography Books

Speedy Publishing LLC
40 E. Main St. #1156
Newark, DE 19711
www.speedypublishing.com
Copyright 2017

All Rights reserved. No part of this book may be reproduced or used in any way or form or by any means whether electronic or mechanical, this means that you cannot record or photocopy any material ideas or tips that are provided in this book

Who was St. Francis of Assisi? Why did he leave a life of wealth to serve God? Read on and learn more about this amazing man.

A WILD YOUNG MAN

The man we know as Francis of Assisi was born around 1181 in Italy. His father was very rich and had land around the town of Assisi, and his mother came from France. Although the child's name was Giovanni, his father started calling him Francesco ("the Frenchman"), and the nickname stuck.

House of Francis of Assisi

Parents of St. Francis

The family was very well off. Francis' father's lands and his cloth business meant that the family had a good home and all luxuries of the times. It seems that Francis was spoiled as a child, and got anything he wanted.

Francis was not a good student and did not pay attention in school. He left school without graduating and went to work for his father—and he wasn't a very good worker, either. The cloth business bored him.

Painting of St. Francis

As a teenager, Francis liked to party. He liked fine food and drinking wine and he stayed out late with his friends. People thought he was charming and handsome, but also vain.

During the day he spent more time practicing archery, riding horses and wrestling than he did learning how to run the family business. His goal in life was to be a famous knight, a military hero. You can read more about what it took to follow that career in the Baby Professor book How to Become a Knight.

A SOLDIER'S LIFE

In 1202, when Francis was about 21, a war started between Assisi and another city, Perugia. Francis joined the cavalry of Assisi. This indicates how wealthy his family was: knights and mounted fighters had to provide and support their own horses, and grooms and servants to take care of the horses, weapons, and armor. Only people from wealthy families could afford the equipment and the training to become mounted fighters.

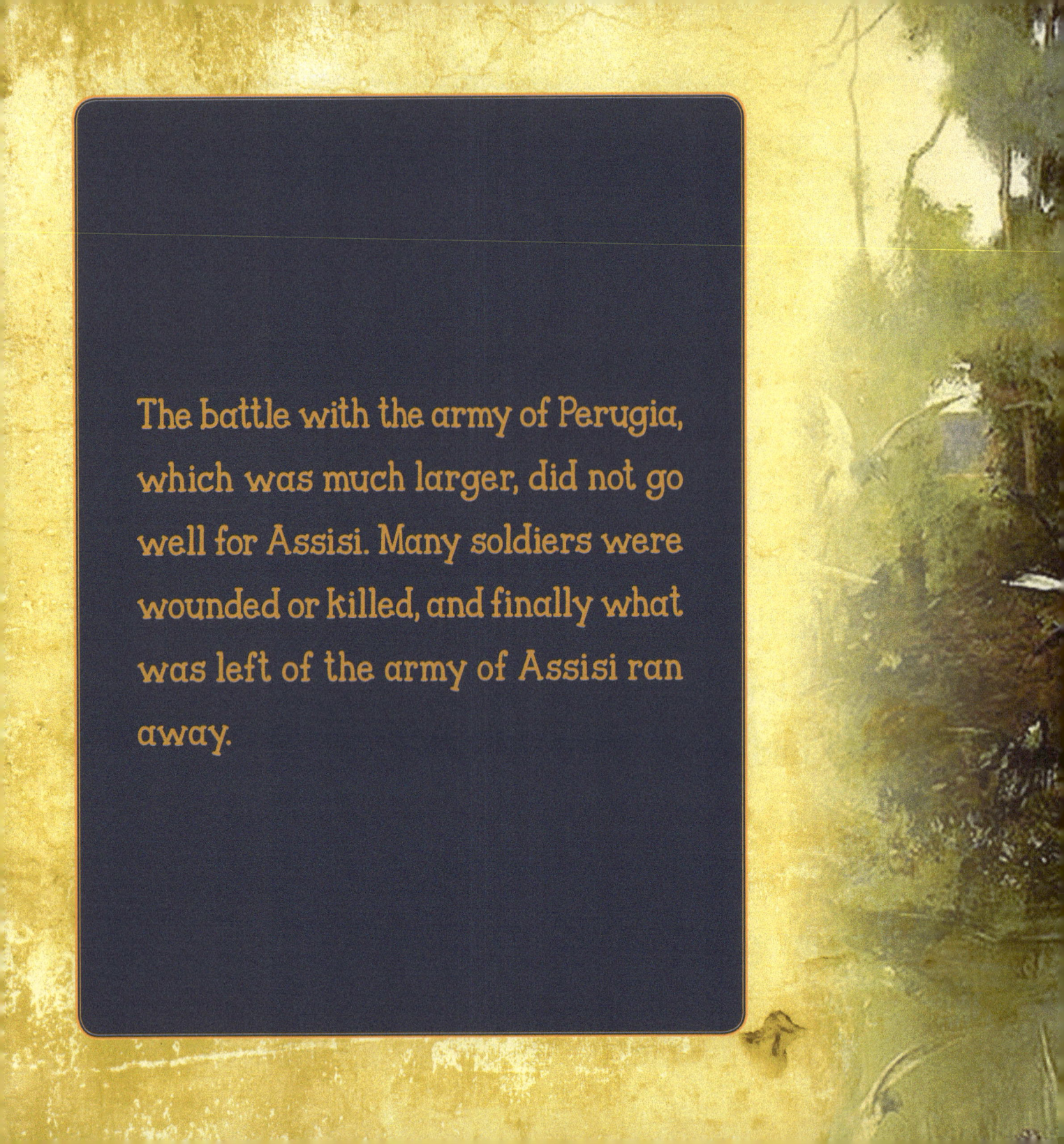

The battle with the army of Perugia, which was much larger, did not go well for Assisi. Many soldiers were wounded or killed, and finally what was left of the army of Assisi ran away.

St. Francis of Assisi

Most of the wounded or captured soldiers from Assisi were put to death right away. This was usually what happened in those days. But rich prisoners were allowed to live, because the army that captured them wanted to make some money by selling them back to their families. Francis, in fine clothing and brand-new armor, was obviously the son of a wealthy family, so Perugia held him as a prisoner.

Francis and the other wealthy captives were put in a prison underground while the terms of their release were worked out. The prison was dark and damp, and Francis may have caught a disease in the year he spent there. He also started experiencing visions; later he said these were the first messages to him from God.

Francis finally was ransomed and able to come home in 1203. He was no longer the carefree teenager with grand plans. He was physically weak, unwell in his body, and deeply troubled in his mind by what he had seen and experienced. Although he did not die in his one battle, he was severely wounded by it in body and soul.

TURNING TOWARD GOD

Sometime after his return home, Francis was riding a horse through the countryside near Assisi. He met a leper, a man suffering from a terrible skin disease for which, at that time, there was no cure. The teenage Francis, son of a comfortable house, would have ridden right by the man.

But the new Francis saw the image of Jesus in this man. He got off the horse and hugged and kissed the man, embracing his weakness and illness with love.

After this encounter, Francis felt a sense of freedom. He lost all interest in the wealthy life in which he had grown up. He started searching for how he could do something that would please God, and that would make a life of more meaning than the life he had lived to this point.

Francis gave up all the pleasures and comforts of a wealthy life. He said he heard the voice of God telling him to rebuild a ruined church and to embrace a life of poverty.

Francis started working on the ruins of the church by hand, by himself. When he was not doing that, he would walk through the countryside and talk to people about living a life that Jesus would want them to live. Some people laughed at him, or even threw things at him or beat him.

But other people became fascinated with how Francis was trying to live and what he was trying to do. His focus on doing God's will, instead of trying to get richer or more powerful, started to attract followers. Soon he had a community of a dozen people living, working, and begging for food with him.

At one point, Francis sold his horse and some cloth from his father's business to help pay for the repairs to the church. His father was furious and took him to see the local bishop. The bishop told Francis to give back the money. Francis not only gave back the money; he took off his clothes and gave them back to his father as well. He severed all ties with his family and its wealth.

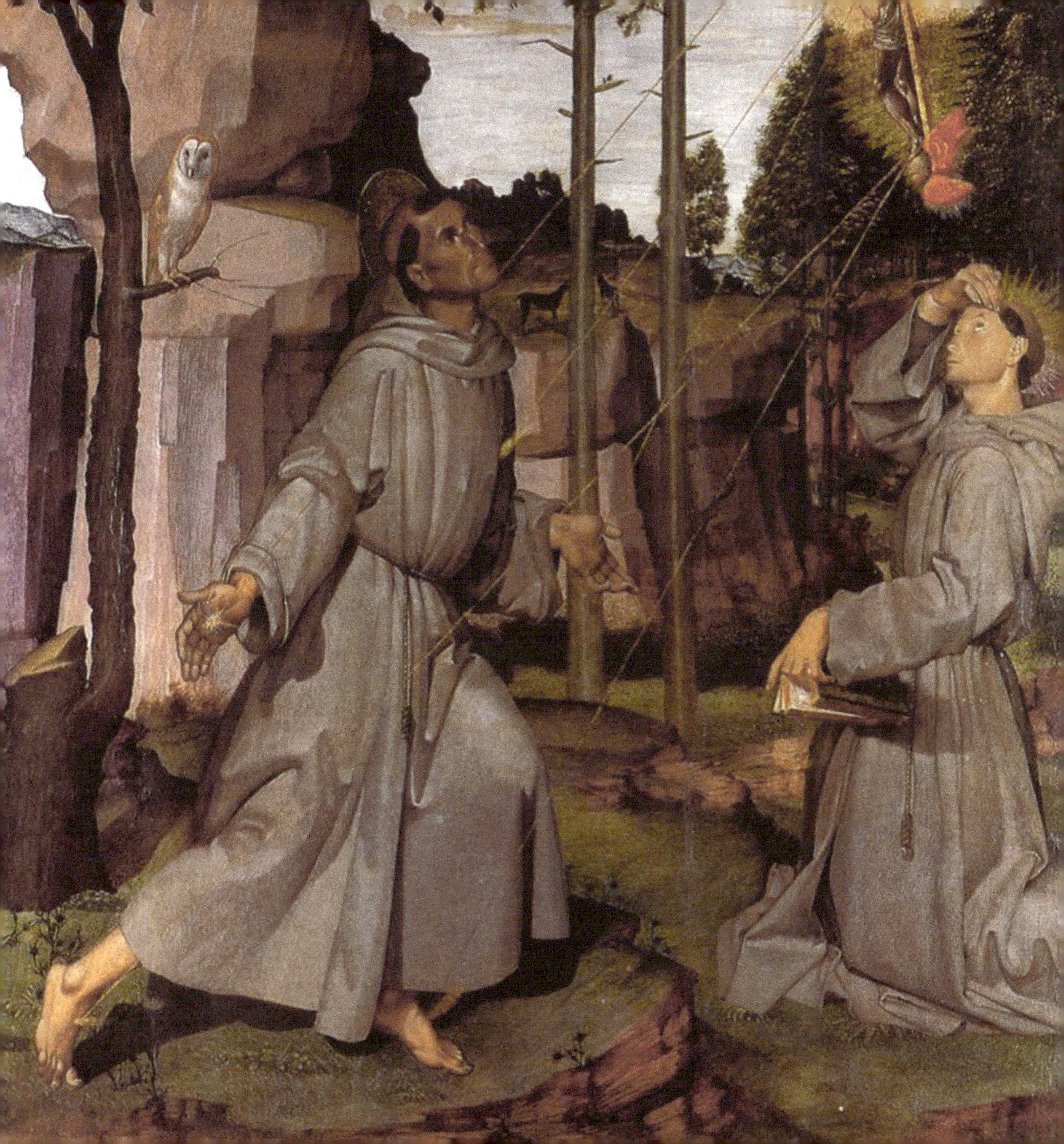

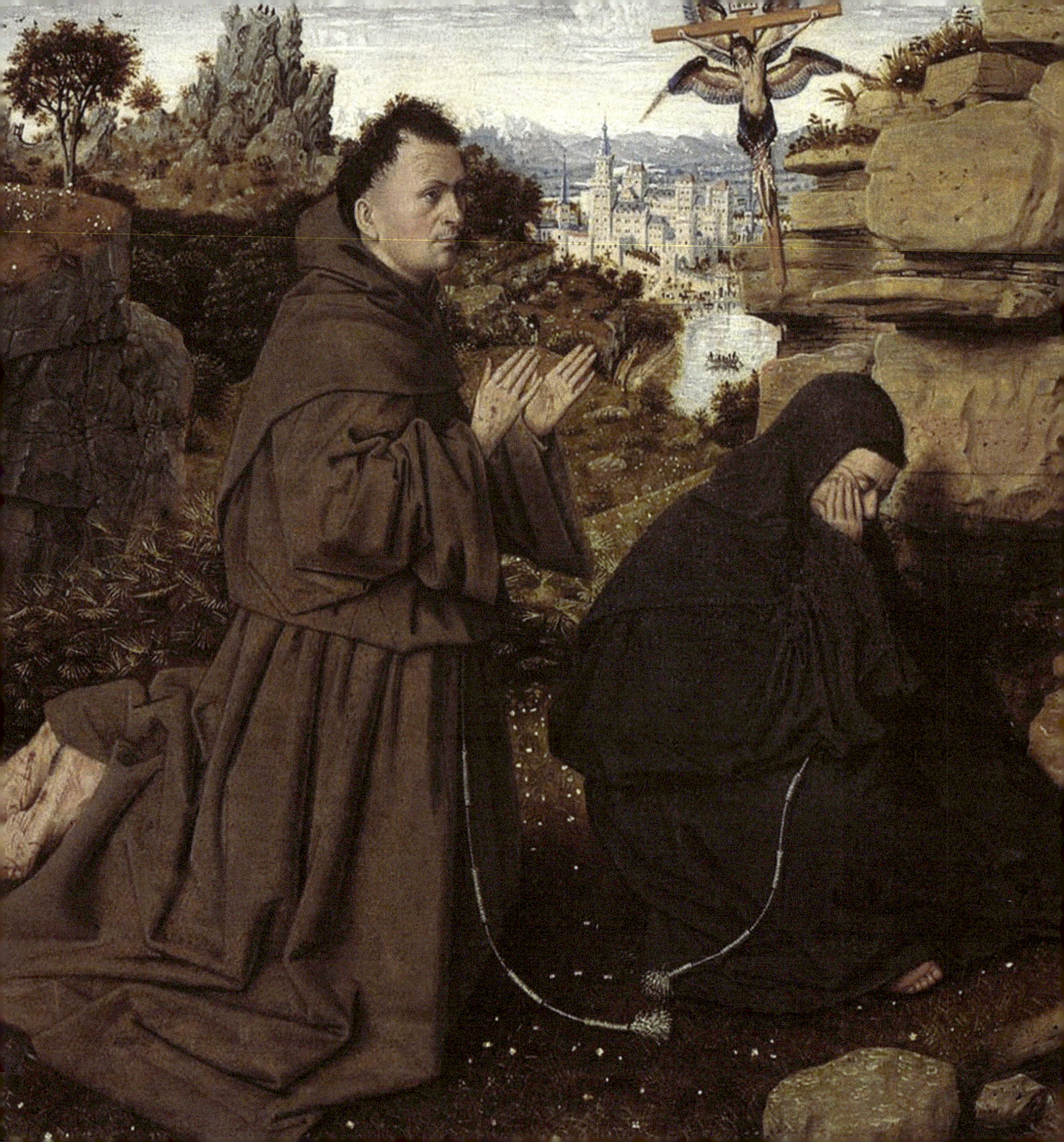

GOD'S FOOL

The bishop found a workman's clothing, a sort of long shirt, and gave it to Francis. This clothing, with a rope around the waist for a belt and a simple pair of sandals, became the basis of the clothing of Francis and his followers.

At this time, the Christian church in Italy and much of Europe was very powerful and wealthy. Just as most countries had a king and a few nobles who had most of the money and power, in the church a few powerful men in top positions used a lot of donations to the church for their own comfort or to meddle in political matters. Most church-goers were very poor, but most clergy lived, wore clothes, and ate in a way that only rich people could in that time.

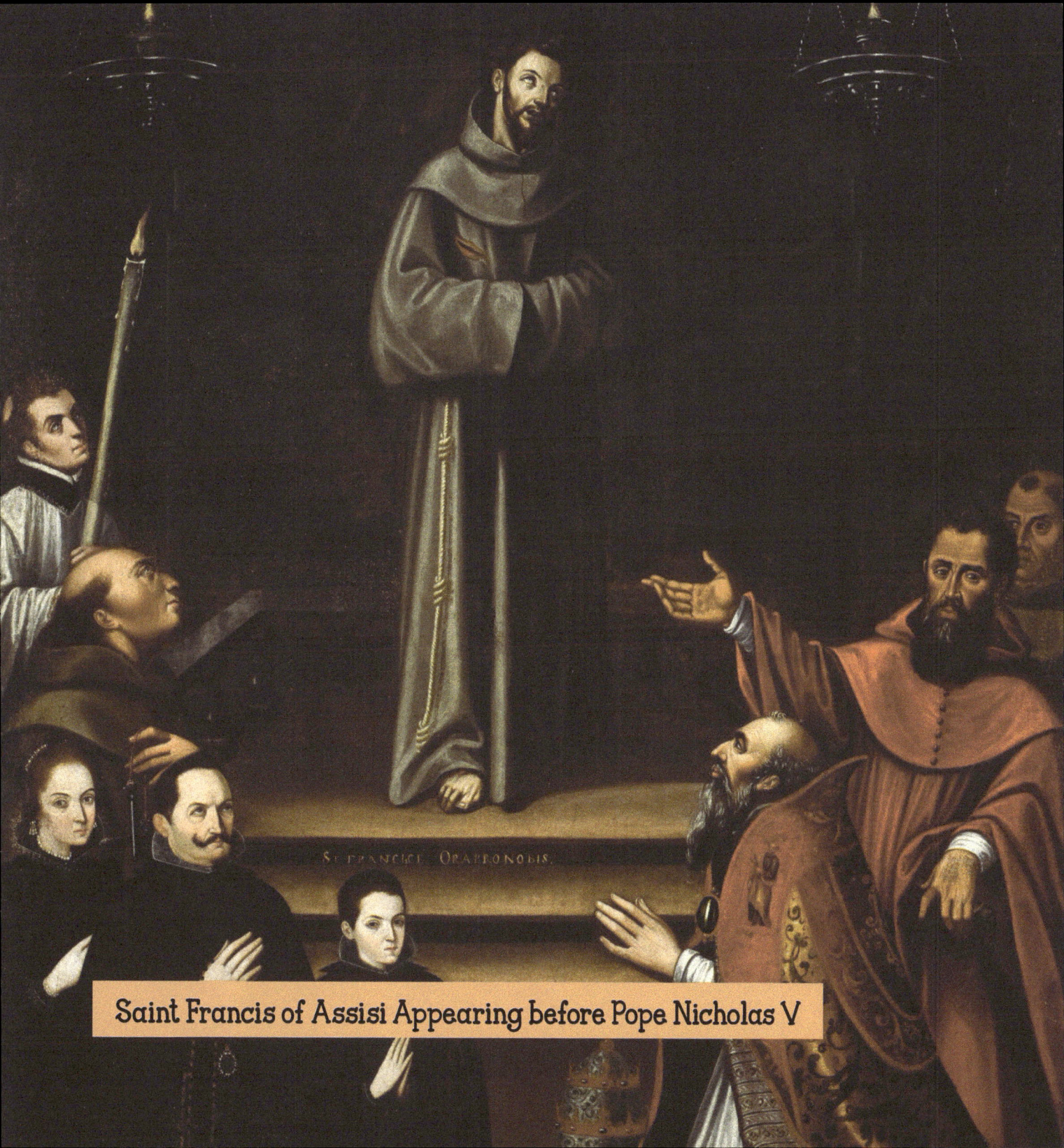

Saint Francis of Assisi Appearing before Pope Nicholas V

Saint John the Baptist and Saint Francis of Assisi

Francis started a campaign to get all the priests, and the whole church, to give up its addiction to money and power. He began to preach and talk to people about how the whole church should live the way Jesus lived, not live for money or glory.

The followers of Francis started going out to preach also, and many people became inspired by his message. His followers became an order known as the Franciscan friars. They spent their energy on sharing the good news and helping the poor.

Franciscan Friars

St. Francis of Assisi Receiving the Stigmata

At one point, Francis decided to ask God for a sign about what he should do. Three times he put a Bible on the altar of the church he had repaired and let it flop open to a random page. Then he closed his eyes and put a finger down on the page. Each time, the Bible was open to a passage about leaving earthly things behind and following Jesus.

Francis went from village to village, preaching to anybody who would listen about how to live a godly life. If nobody wanted to listen to him, he would sometimes preach to the animals. People laughed at that and said that Francis was "God's fool", and Francis gladly accepted that insult as a compliment.

Saint Francis Preaching to Animals

St Francis receiving the Stigmata

In 1224, when he was about 43, Francis reported that he had had a vision of Jesus hanging on the cross. After that vision, he had marks on his hands and feet, and on his side, as if Francis had received the same wounds that Jesus had when Jesus was crucified.

DEATH AND LEGACY

More and more people began to come to hear Francis and his followers, and his message spread rapidly. However he was in poor health and became weaker and weaker. He finally died in 1226, at the age of 44.

Death of St Francis

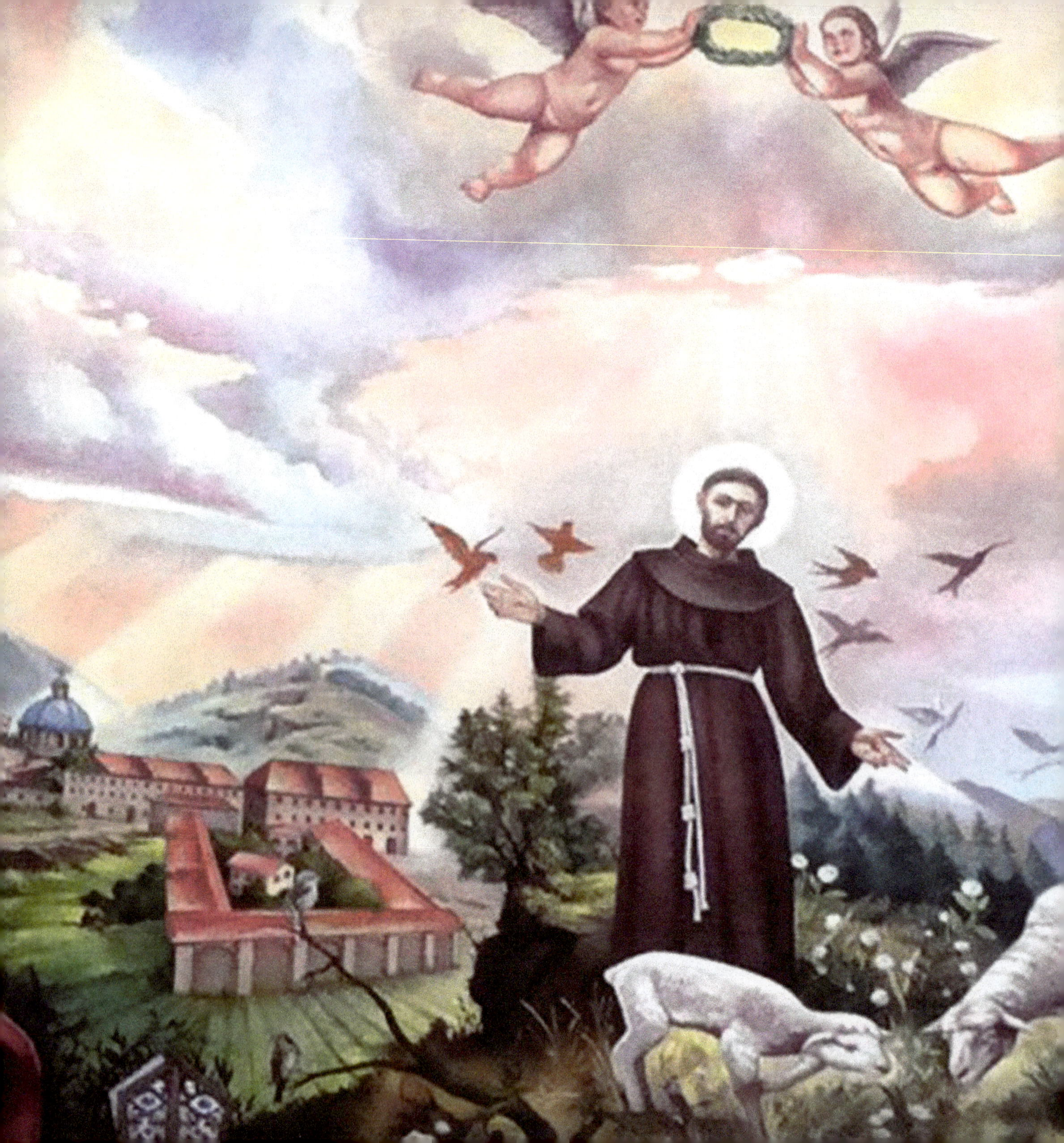

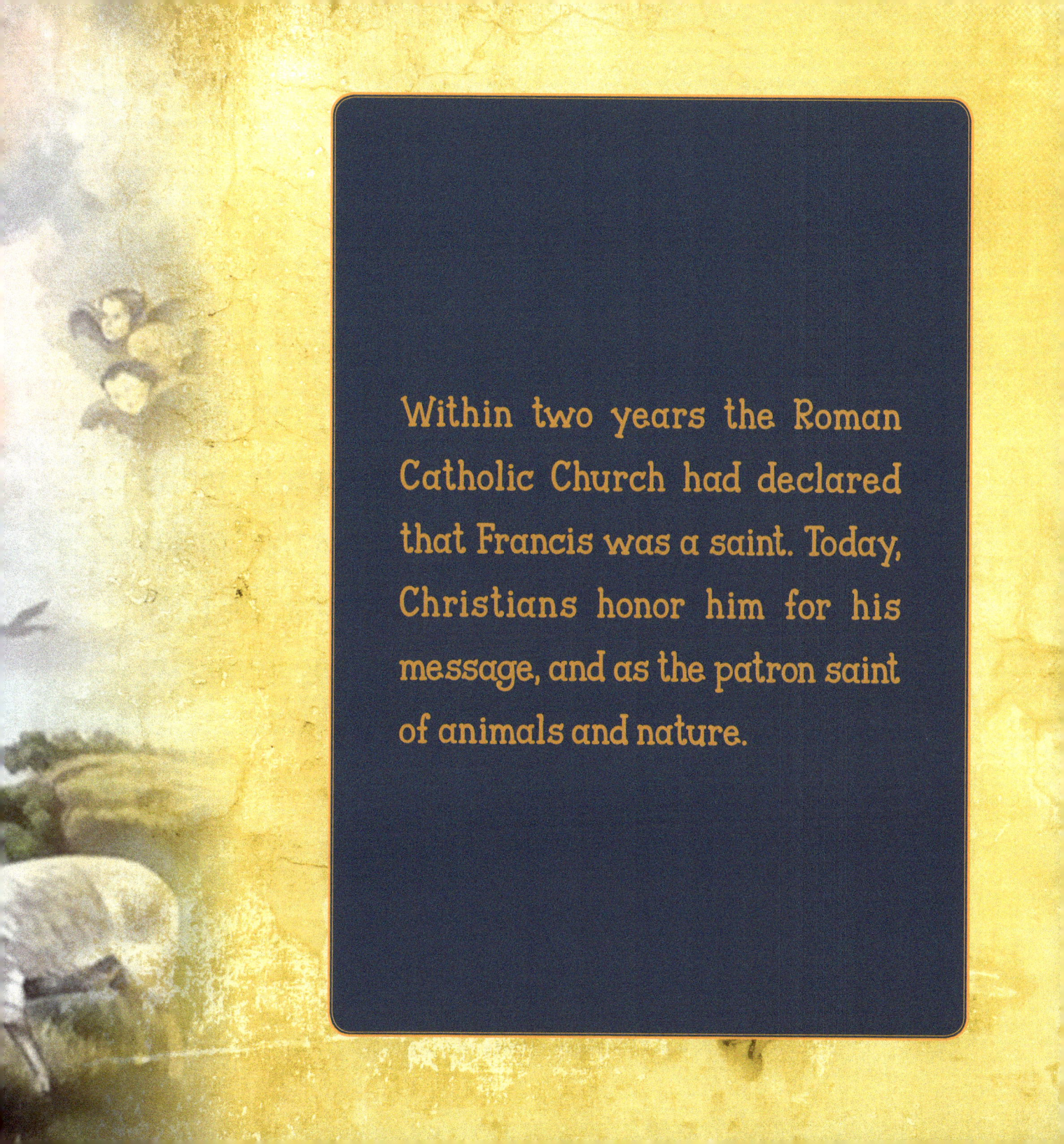

Within two years the Roman Catholic Church had declared that Francis was a saint. Today, Christians honor him for his message, and as the patron saint of animals and nature.

The Franciscan order was part of a great effort to reform the Christian church, and in many ways it succeeded. The order has also had great success over the centuries in helping the poor, the sick, and the dying, and in avoiding laying up great wealth for the order or for its members.

Franciscan order

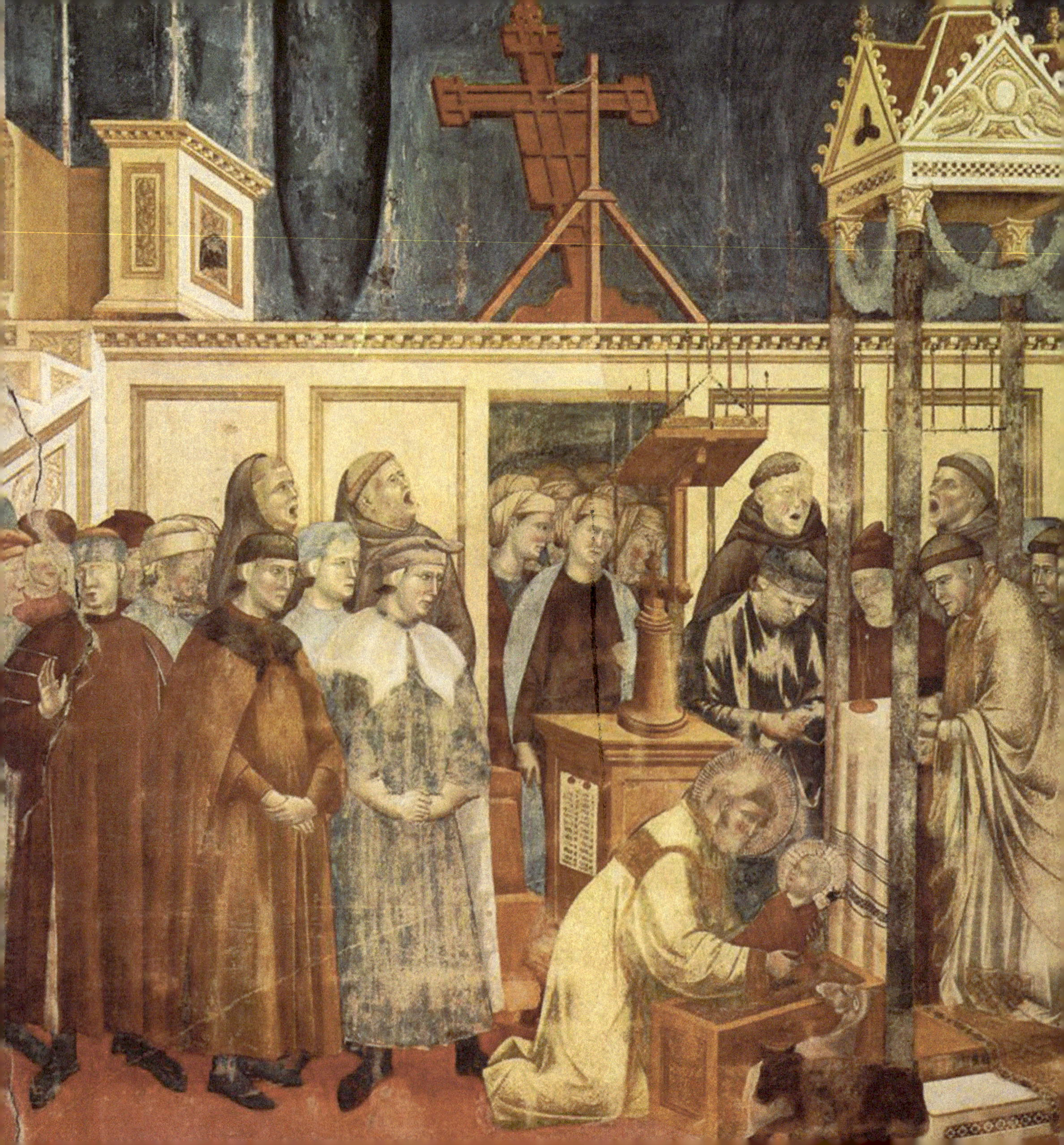

Here's a small legacy from Francis: in 1223, before Christmas, he had the idea of putting in the church in the town of Greccio a manger like the one the baby Jesus would have slept in after he was born in Bethlehem. You may see around Christmas time manger scenes outside of churches, and small manger scenes, with tiny animals and people, in churches and private houses. This practice comes from Francis' idea of a way to remember what really happened on the first Christmas.

PEOPLE CAN CHANGE THE WORLD

Francis devoted his life to a great idea, and many other people have done the same to make the world better. Read Baby Professor books, like Marquis de Lafayette: The Hero of Two Worlds, to learn about other great and devoted people.

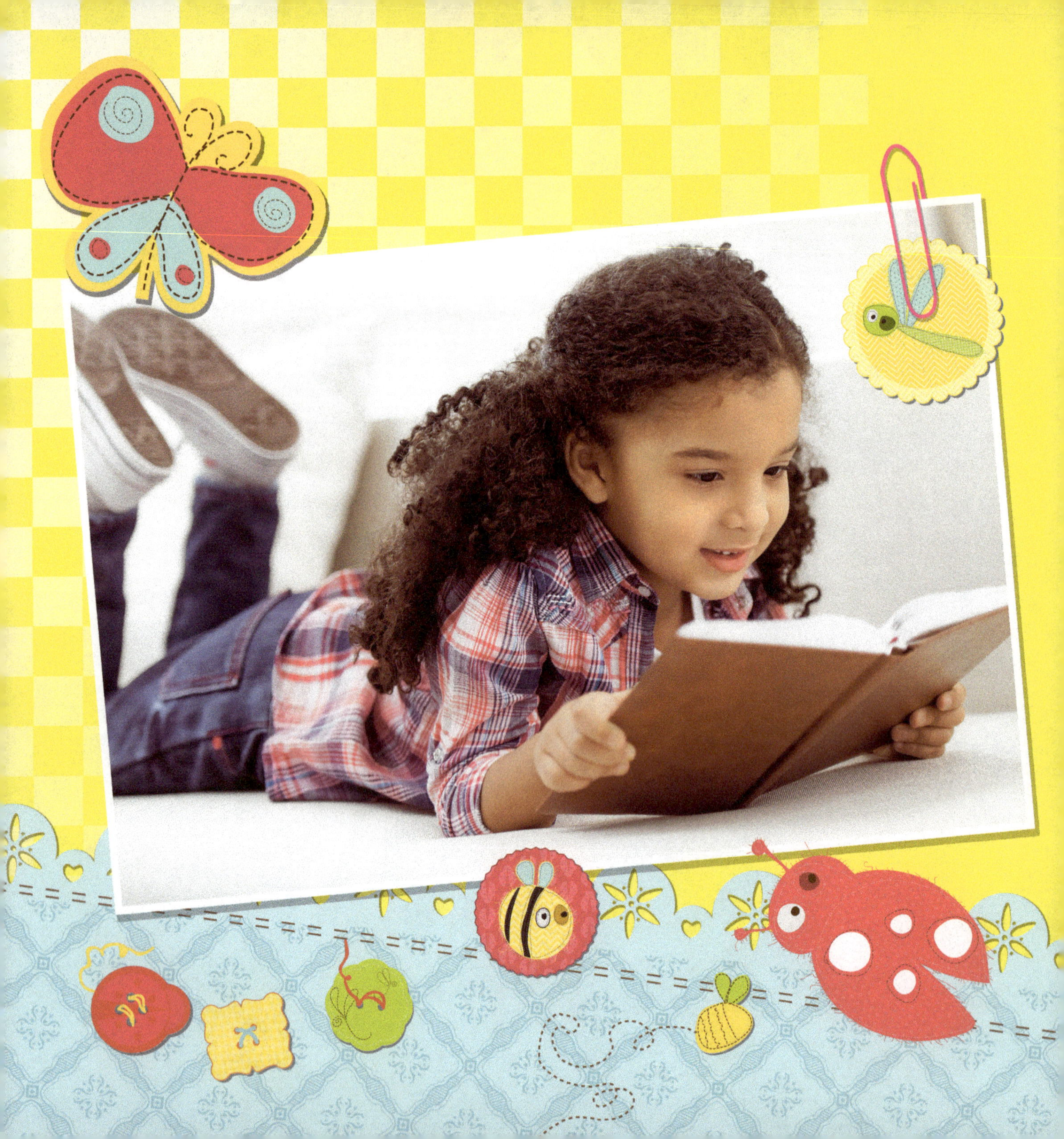

Visit

BABY PROFESSOR
EDUCATION KIDS

www.BabyProfessorBooks.com

to download Free Baby Professor eBooks and view our catalog of new and exciting Children's Books

Lightning Source UK Ltd.
Milton Keynes UK
UKHW050158310321
381275UK00005B/26

9 781541 913813